Regime Strategic Intent

Key Findings

Saddam Husayn so dominated the Iraqi Regime that its strategic intent was his alone. He wanted to end sanctions while preserving the capability to reconstitute his weapons of mass destruction (WMD) when sanctions were lifted.

- *Saddam totally dominated the Regime's strategic decision making.* He initiated most of the strategic thinking upon which decisions were made, whether in matters of war and peace (such as invading Kuwait), maintaining WMD as a national strategic goal, or on how Iraq was to position itself in the international community. Loyal dissent was discouraged and constructive variations to the implementation of his wishes on strategic issues were rare. Saddam was the Regime in a strategic sense and his intent became Iraq's strategic policy.

- *Saddam's primary goal from 1991 to 2003 was to have UN sanctions lifted, while maintaining the security of the Regime.* He sought to balance the need to cooperate with UN inspections—to gain support for lifting sanctions—with his intention to preserve Iraq's intellectual capital for WMD with a minimum of foreign intrusiveness and loss of face. Indeed, this remained the goal to the end of the Regime, as the starting of any WMD program, conspicuous or otherwise, risked undoing the progress achieved in eroding sanctions and jeopardizing a political end to the embargo and international monitoring.

- *The introduction of the Oil-For-Food program (OFF) in late 1996 was a key turning point for the Regime.* OFF rescued Baghdad's economy from a terminal decline created by sanctions. The Regime quickly came to see that OFF could be corrupted to acquire foreign exchange both to further undermine sanctions and to provide the means to enhance dual-use infrastructure and potential WMD-related development.

- *By 2000-2001, Saddam had managed to mitigate many of the effects of sanctions and undermine their international support.* Iraq was within striking distance of a *de facto* end to the sanctions regime, both in terms of oil exports and the trade embargo, by the end of 1999.

Saddam wanted to recreate Iraq's WMD capability—which was essentially destroyed in 1991—after sanctions were removed and Iraq's economy stabilized, but probably with a different mix of capabilities to that which previously existed. Saddam aspired to develop a nuclear capability—in an incremental fashion, irrespective of international pressure and the resulting economic risks—but he intended to focus on ballistic missile and tactical chemical warfare (CW) capabilities.

- *Iran was the pre-eminent motivator of this policy.* All senior level Iraqi officials considered Iran to be Iraq's principal enemy in the region. The wish to balance Israel and acquire status and influence in the Arab world were also considerations, but secondary.

- *Iraq Survey Group (ISG) judges that events in the 1980s and early 1990s shaped Saddam's belief in the value of WMD.* In Saddam's view, WMD helped to save the Regime multiple times. He believed that during the Iran-Iraq war chemical weapons had halted Iranian ground offensives and that ballistic missile attacks on Tehran had broken its political will. Similarly, during Desert Storm, Saddam believed WMD had deterred Coalition Forces from pressing their attack beyond the goal of freeing Kuwait. WMD had even played a role in crushing the Shi'a revolt in the south following the 1991 cease-fire.

- *The former Regime had no formal written strategy or plan for the revival of WMD after sanctions.* Neither was there an identifiable group of WMD policy makers or planners separate from Saddam. Instead, his lieutenants understood WMD revival was his goal from their long association with Saddam and his infrequent, but firm, verbal comments and directions to them.

Note on Methodological Approach

Interviews with former Regime officials who were active in Iraq's governing, economic, security, and intelligence structures were critical to ISG's assessment of the former Regime's WMD strategy. *While some detainees' statements were made to minimize their involvement or culpability leading to potential prosecution, in some cases those who were interviewed spoke relatively candidly and at length about the Regime's strategic intent.*

- *ISG analysts—because of unprecedented access to detainees—undertook interviews of national policy makers, the leadership of the intelligence and security services, and Qusay's inner circle, as well as concentrated debriefs of core Regime leaders in custody, to identify cross-Regime issues and perceptions.*

- *As part of the effort aimed at the core leadership, analysts also gave detainees "homework" to give them more opportunity to discuss in writing various aspects of former Regime strategy. Many of these responses were lengthy and detailed. Secretary of the President, 'Abd Hamid Al Khatab Al Nasiri, Deputy Prime Minister Tariq 'Aziz 'Aysa, and Minister of Military Industry 'Abd-al-Tawab 'Abdallah Al Mullah Huwaysh answered questions in writing several times, providing information on both the former Regime and the mindset of those who ran it.*

- *Saddam's debriefer was fully aware of ISG's information needs and developed a strategy to elicit candid answers and insights into Saddam's personality and role in strategy-related issues. Remarks from the debriefer are included.*

- *Analysts also used working groups to study themes and trends—such as intelligence and security service activity, weaponization, dual-use/break-out capabilities and timeline analysis—that cut across ISG's functional teams, as well as to pool efforts to debrief members of the core leadership.*

Analysts used subsource development and document exploitation to crosscheck detainee testimony, leverage detainees in debriefs, and to fill gaps in information. *For example, analysts interviewing Huwaysh gained insights into his personality from subsources, while translated technical and procurement-related documents were critical to verifying the accuracy of his testimony. Likewise, we confronted Vice President Taha Yasin Ramadan Al Jizrawi with a captured document indicating his major role in allocating oil contracts and he divulged details on corruption stemming from the UN's OFF program.*

Nonetheless, the interview process had several shortcomings. *Detainees were very concerned about their fate and therefore would not be willing to implicate themselves in sensitive matters of interest such as WMD, in light of looming prosecutions. Debriefers noted the use of passive interrogation resistance techniques collectively by a large number of detainees to avoid their involvement or knowledge of sensitive issues; place blame or knowledge with individuals who were not in a position to contradict the detainee's statements, such as deceased individuals or individuals who were not in custody or who had fled the country; and provide debriefers with previously known information. However, the reader should keep in mind the Arab proverb: "Even a liar tells many truths."*

Some former Regime officials, such as 'Ali Hasan Al Majid Al Tikriti (Chemical 'Ali), never gave substantial information, despite speaking colorfully and at length. He never discussed actions, which would implicate him in a crime. Moreover, for some aspects of the Regime's WMD strategy, like the role of the Military Industrialization Commission (MIC), analysts could only speak with a few senior-level officials, which limited ISG's assessment to the perspectives of these individuals.

Former Iraqi Regime Officials Varied in Their Level of Cooperation

The quality of cooperation and assistance provided to ISG by former senior Iraqi Regime officials in custody varied widely. Some obstructed all attempts to elicit information on WMD and illicit activities of the former Regime. Others, however, were keen to help clarify every issue, sometimes to the point of self-incrimination. The two extremes of cooperation are epitomized by 'Ali Hasan Al Majid—a key Presidential Adviser and RCC member—and Sabir 'Abd-al-Aziz Husayn Al Duri, a former Lieutenant General who served in both the Directorate of General Military Intelligence and the Iraqi Intelligence Service. 'Ali Hasan Al Majid was loquacious on many subjects, but remained adamant in denying any involvement in the use of CW in attacks on the Kurds and dissembling in any discussion of the subject. His circumlocution extends to most other sensitive subjects of Regime behavior. By contrast, Sabir has been forthcoming to the point of direct association with a wide range of Iraqi activities, including the management of Kuwaiti prisoners, the organization of assassinations abroad by the former Iraqi Intelligence Service (IIS), and the torture of political prisoners.

Regime Finance and Procurement

Key Findings

Throughout the 1990s and up to OIF (March 2003), Saddam focused on one set of objectives: the survival of himself, his Regime, and his legacy. To secure those objectives, Saddam needed to exploit Iraqi oil assets, to portray a strong military capability to deter internal and external threats, and to foster his image as an Arab leader. Saddam recognized that the reconstitution of Iraqi WMD enhanced both his security and image. Consequently, Saddam needed to end UN-imposed sanctions to fulfill his goals.

Saddam severely under estimated the economic and military costs of invading Iran in 1980 and Kuwait in 1990, as well as underestimating the subsequent international condemnation of his invasion of Kuwait. He did not anticipate this condemnation, nor the subsequent imposition, comprehensiveness, severity, and longevity of UN sanctions. His initial belief that UN sanctions would not last, resulting in his country's economic decline, changed by 1998 when the UNSC did not lift sanctions after he believed resolutions were fulfilled. Although Saddam had reluctantly accepted the UN's Oil for Food (OFF) program by 1996, he soon recognized its economic value and additional opportunities for further manipulation and influence of the UNSC Iraq 661 Sanctions Committee member states. Therefore, he resigned himself to the continuation of UN sanctions understanding that they would become a "paper tiger" regardless of continued US resolve to maintain them.

Throughout sanctions, Saddam continually directed his advisors to formulate and implement strategies, policies, and methods to terminate the UN's sanctions regime established by UNSCR 661. The Regime devised an effective diplomatic and economic strategy of generating revenue and procuring illicit goods utilizing the Iraqi intelligence, banking, industrial, and military apparatus that eroded United Nations' member states and other international players' resolve to enforce compliance, while capitalizing politically on its humanitarian crisis.

- From Saddam's perspective, UN sanctions hindered his ability to rule Iraq with complete authority and autonomy. In the long run, UN sanctions also interfered with his efforts to establish a historic legacy. *According to Saddam and his senior advisors, the UN, at the behest of the US, placed an economic strangle hold on Iraq.* The UN controlled Saddam's main source of revenue (oil exports) and determined what Iraq could import.

- UN sanctions curbed Saddam's ability to import weapons, technology, and expertise into Iraq. Sanctions also limited his ability to finance his military, intelligence, and security forces to deal with his perceived and real external threats.

- In short, Saddam considered UN sanctions as a form of economic war and the UN's OFF program and Northern and Southern Watch Operations as campaigns of that larger economic war orchestrated by the US and UK. His evolving strategy centered on breaking free of UN sanctions in order to liberate his economy from the economic strangle-hold so he could continue to pursue his political and personal objectives.

One aspect of Saddam's strategy of unhinging the UN's sanctions against Iraq, centered on Saddam's efforts to influence certain UN SC permanent members, such as Russia, France, and China and some nonpermanent (Syria, Ukraine) members to end UN sanctions. *Under Saddam's orders, the Ministry of Foreign Affairs (MFA) formulated and implemented a strategy aimed at these UNSC members and international public opinion with the purpose of ending UN sanctions and undermining its subsequent OFF program by diplomatic and economic means.* At a minimum, Saddam wanted to divide the five permanent members and foment international public support of Iraq at the UN and throughout the world by a savvy public relations campaign and an extensive diplomatic effort.

Another element of this strategy involved circumventing UN sanctions and the OFF program by means of "Protocols" or government-to-government economic trade agreements. Protocols allowed Saddam to generate a large amount of revenue outside the purview of the UN. The successful implementation of the Protocols, continued oil smuggling efforts, and the manipulation of UN OFF contracts emboldened Saddam to pursue his military reconstitution efforts starting in 1997 and peaking in 2001. These efforts covered conventional arms, dual-use goods acquisition, and some WMD-related programs.

- Once money began to flow into Iraq, the Regime's authorities, aided by foreign companies and some foreign governments, devised and implemented methods and techniques to procure illicit goods from foreign suppliers.

- To implement its procurement efforts, Iraq under Saddam, created a network of Iraqi front companies, some with close relationships to high-ranking foreign government officials. These foreign government officials, in turn, worked through their respective ministries, state-run companies and ministry-sponsored front companies, to procure illicit goods, services, and technologies for Iraq's WMD-related, conventional arms, and/or dual-use goods programs.

- ***The Regime financed these government-sanctioned programs by several illicit revenue streams that amassed more that $11 billion from the early 1990s to OIF outside the UN-approved methods.*** The most profitable stream concerned Protocols or government-to-government agreements that generated over $7.5 billion for Saddam. Iraq earned an additional $2 billion from kickbacks or surcharges associated with the UN's OFF program; $990 million from oil "cash sales" or smuggling; and another $230 million from other surcharge impositions.

Analysis of Iraqi Financial Data

The Iraqi revenue analysis presented in this report is based on government documents and financial databases, spreadsheets, and other records obtained from SOMO, the Iraqi Ministry of Oil, and the Central Bank of Iraq (CBI), and other Ministries. These sources appear to be of good quality and consistent with other pre- and post-Operation Iraqi Freedom information. All Iraqi revenue data and derived figures in this report have been calculated in current dollars.

Saddam directed the Regime's key ministries and governmental agencies to devise and implement strategies, policies, and techniques to discredit the UN sanctions, harass UN personnel in Iraq, and discredit the US. At the same time, according to reporting, he also wanted to obfuscate Iraq's refusal to reveal the nature of its WMD and WMD-related programs, their capabilities, and his intentions.

- ***Saddam used the IIS to undertake the most sensitive procurement missions. Consequently, the IIS facilitated the import of UN sanctioned and dual-use goods into Iraq through countries like Syria, Jordan, Belarus and Turkey.***

- The IIS had representatives in most of Iraq's embassies in these foreign countries using a variety of official covers. One type of cover was the "commercial attaches" that were sent to make contacts with foreign businesses. The attaches set up front companies, facilitated the banking process and transfers of funds as determined, and approved by the senior officials within the Government.

- The MFA played a critical role in facilitating Iraq's procurement of military goods, dual-use goods pertaining to WMD, transporting cash and other valuable goods earned by illicit oil revenue, and forming and implementing a diplomatic strategy to end UN sanctions and the subsequent UN OFF program by nefarious means.

- Saddam used the Ministry of Higher Education and Scientific Research (MHESR) through its universities and research programs to maintain, develop, and acquire expertise, to advance or preserve existent research projects and developments, and to procure goods prohibited by UN SC sanctions.

- The Ministry of Oil (MoO) controlled the oil voucher distribution program that used oil to influence UN members to support Iraq's goals. ***Saddam personally approved and removed all names of voucher recipi-***

ents. He made all modifications to the list, adding or deleting names at will. Other senior Iraqi leaders could nominate or recommend an individual or organization to be added or subtracted from the voucher list, and ad hoc allocation committees met to review and update the allocations.

Iraq under Saddam successfully devised various methods to acquire and import items prohibited under UN sanctions. *Numerous Iraqi and foreign trade intermediaries disguised illicit items, hid the identity of the end user, and/or changed the final destination of the commodity to get it to the region.* For a cut of the profits, these trade intermediaries moved, and in many cases smuggled, the prohibited items through land, sea, and air entry points along the Iraqi border.

By mid-2000 the exponential growth of Iraq's illicit revenue, increased international sympathy for Iraq's humanitarian plight, and increased complicity by Iraqi's neighbors led elements within Saddam's Regime to boast that the UN sanctions were slowly eroding. In July 2000, the ruling Iraqi Ba'athist paper, Al-Thawrah, claimed victory over UN sanctions, stating that Iraq was accelerating its pace to develop its national economy despite the UN "blockade." In August 2001, Iraqi Foreign Minister Sabri stated in an Al-Jazirah TV interview that UN sanctions efforts had collapsed at the same time Baghdad had been making steady progress on its economic, military, Arab relations, and international affairs.

- Companies in Syria, Jordan, Lebanon, Turkey, UAE, and Yemen assisted Saddam with the acquisition of prohibited items through deceptive trade practices. In the case of Syria and Yemen, this included support from agencies or personnel within the government itself.

- Numerous ministries in Saddam's Regime facilitated the smuggling of illicit goods through Iraq's borders, ports, and airports. The Iraqi Intelligence Service (IIS) and the Military Industiralization Commission (MIC), however, were directly responsible for skirting UN monitoring and importing prohibited items for Saddam.

Delivery Systems

Key Findings

Since the early 1970s, Iraq has consistently sought to acquire an effective long-range weapons delivery capability, and by 1991 Baghdad had purchased the missiles and infrastructure that would form the basis for nearly all of its future missile system developments. The Soviet Union was a key supplier of missile hardware and provided 819 Scud-B missiles and ground support equipment.

Iraq's experiences with long-range delivery systems in the Iran/Iraq war were a vital lesson to Iraqi President Saddam Husayn. The successful Iraqi response to the Iranian long-range bombardment of Baghdad, leading to the War of the Cities, probably saved Saddam.

By 1991, Iraq had successfully demonstrated its ability to modify some of its delivery systems to increase their range and to develop WMD dissemination options, with the Al Husayn being a first step in this direction. The next few years of learning and experiments confirmed that the Regime's goal was for an effective long-range WMD delivery capability and demonstrated the resourcefulness of Iraq's scientists and technicians.

Iraq failed in its efforts to acquire longer-range delivery systems to replace inventory exhausted in the Iran/Iraq war. This was a forcing function that drove Iraq to develop indigenous delivery system production capabilities.

Desert Storm and subsequent UN resolutions and inspections brought many of Iraq's delivery system programs to a halt. While much of Iraq's long-range missile inventory and production infrastructure was eliminated, Iraq until late 1991 kept some items hidden to assist future reconstitution of the force. This decision and Iraq's intransigence during years of inspection left many UN questions unresolved.

- Coalition airstrikes effectively targeted much of Iraq's delivery systems infrastructure, and UN inspections dramatically impeded further developments of long-range ballistic missiles.

- *It appears to have taken time, but Iraq eventually realized that sanctions were not going to end quickly.* This forced Iraq to sacrifice its long-range delivery force in an attempt to bring about a quick end to the sanctions.

- After the flight of Husayn Kamil in 1995, Iraq admitted that it had hidden Scud-variant missiles and components to aid future reconstitution but asserted that these items had been unilaterally destroyed by late 1991. The UN could not verify these claims and thereafter became more wary of Iraq's admissions and instituted a Regime of more intrusive inspections.

- *The Iraq Survey Group (ISG) has uncovered no evidence Iraq retained Scud-variant missiles, and debriefings of Iraqi officials in addition to some documentation suggest that Iraq did not retain such missiles after 1991.*

While other WMD programs were strictly prohibited, the UN permitted Iraq to develop and possess delivery systems provided their range did not exceed 150 km. This freedom allowed Iraq to keep its scientists and technicians employed and to keep its infrastructure and manufacturing base largely intact by pursuing programs nominally in compliance with the UN limitations. *This positioned Iraq for a potential breakout capability.*

- Between 1991 and 1998, Iraq had declared development programs underway for liquid- and solid-propellant ballistic missiles and unmanned aerial vehicles (UAVs).

Iraq's decisions in 1996 to accept the Oil-For-Food program (OFF) and later in 1998 to cease cooperation with UNSCOM and IAEA spurred a period of increased activity in delivery systems development. The pace of ongoing missile programs accelerated, and the Regime authorized its scientists to design missiles with ranges in excess of 150 km that, if developed, would have been clear violations of UNSCR 687.

- By 2002, Iraq had provided the liquid-propellant Al Samud II—a program started in 2001—and the solid-propellant Al Fat'h to the military and was pursuing a series of new small UAV systems.

- *ISG uncovered Iraqi plans or designs for three long-range ballistic missiles with ranges from 400 to 1,000 km and for a 1,000-km-range cruise missile, although none of these systems progressed to production and only one reportedly passed the design phase. ISG assesses that these plans demonstrate Saddam's continuing desire—up to the beginning of Operation Iraqi Freedom (OIF)—for a long-range delivery capability.*

Procurements supporting delivery system programs expanded after the 1998 departure of the UN inspectors. Iraq also hired outside expertise to assist its development programs.

- ISG uncovered evidence that technicians and engineers from Russia reviewed the designs and assisted development of the Al Samud II during its rapid evolution. ISG also found that Iraq had entered into negotiations with North Korean and Russian entities for more capable missile systems.

- According to contract information exploited by ISG, Iraq imported at least 380 SA-2/Volga liquid-propellant engines from Poland and possibly Russia or Belarus. While Iraq claims these engines were for the Al Samud II program, the numbers involved appear in excess of immediate requirements, suggesting they could have supported the longer range missiles using clusters of SA-2 engines. Iraq also imported missile guidance and control systems from entities in countries like Belarus, Russia and Federal Republic of Yugoslavia (FRY). (Note: FRY is currently known as Serbia and Montenegro but is referred to as FRY in this section.)

In late 2002 Iraq was under increasing pressure from the international community to allow UN inspectors to return. Iraq in November accepted UNSCR 1441 and invited inspectors back into the country. In December Iraq presented to the UN its Currently Accurate, Full, and Complete Declaration (CAFCD) in response to UNSCR 1441.

- While the CAFCD was judged to be incomplete and a rehash of old information, it did provide details on the Al Samud II, Al Fat'h, new missile-related facilities, and new small UAV designs.

- In February 2003 the UN convened an expert panel to discuss the Al Samud II and Al Fat'h programs, which resulted in the UN's decision to prohibit the Al Samud II and order its destruction. Missile destruction began in early March but was incomplete when the inspectors were withdrawn later that month.

The CAFCD and United Nations Monitoring, Verification, and Inspection Commission (UNMOVIC) inspections provided a brief glimpse into what Iraq had accomplished in four years without an international presence on the ground.

Given Iraq's investments in technology and infrastructure improvements, an effective procurement network, skilled scientists, and designs already on the books for longer range missiles, ISG assesses that Saddam clearly intended to reconstitute long-range delivery systems and that the systems potentially were for WMD.

- Iraq built a new and larger liquid-rocket engine test stand capable, with some modification, of supporting engines or engine clusters larger than the single SA-2 engine used in the Al Samud II.

- Iraq built or refurbished solid-propellant facilities and equipment, including a large propellant mixer, an aging oven, and a casting pit that could support large diameter motors.

- Iraq's investing in studies into new propellants and manufacturing technologies demonstrated its desire for more capable or effective delivery systems.

Nuclear

Key Findings

Iraq Survey Group (ISG) discovered further evidence of the maturity and significance of the pre-1991 Iraqi Nuclear Program but found that Iraq's ability to reconstitute a nuclear weapons program progressively decayed after that date.

- Saddam Husayn ended the nuclear program in 1991 following the Gulf war. ISG found no evidence to suggest concerted efforts to restart the program.

- Although Saddam clearly assigned a high value to the nuclear progress and talent that had been developed up to the 1991 war, the program ended and the intellectual capital decayed in the succeeding years.

Nevertheless, after 1991, Saddam did express his intent to retain the intellectual capital developed during the Iraqi Nuclear Program. Senior Iraqis—several of them from the Regime's inner circle—told ISG they assumed Saddam would restart a nuclear program once UN sanctions ended.

- Saddam indicated that he would develop the weapons necessary to counter any Iranian threat.

Initially, Saddam chose to conceal his nuclear program in its entirety, as he did with Iraq's BW program. Aggressive UN inspections after Desert Storm forced Saddam to admit the existence of the program and destroy or surrender components of the program.

In the wake of Desert Storm, Iraq took steps to conceal key elements of its program and to preserve what it could of the professional capabilities of its nuclear scientific community.

- Baghdad undertook a variety of measures to conceal key elements of its nuclear program from successive UN inspectors, including specific direction by Saddam Husayn to hide and preserve documentation associated with Iraq's nuclear program.

- ISG, for example, uncovered two specific instances in which scientists involved in uranium enrichment kept documents and technology. Although apparently acting on their own, they did so with the belief and anticipation of resuming uranium enrichment efforts in the future.

- Starting around 1992, in a bid to retain the intellectual core of the former weapons program, Baghdad transferred many nuclear scientists to related jobs in the Military Industrial Commission (MIC). The work undertaken by these scientists at the MIC helped them maintain their weapons knowledge base.

As with other WMD areas, Saddam's ambitions in the nuclear area were secondary to his prime objective of ending UN sanctions.

- Iraq, especially after the defection of Husayn Kamil in 1995, sought to persuade the IAEA that Iraq had met the UN's disarmament requirements so sanctions would be lifted.

ISG found a limited number of post-1995 activities that would have aided the reconstitution of the nuclear weapons program once sanctions were lifted.

- The activities of the Iraqi Atomic Energy Commission sustained some talent and limited research with potential relevance to a reconstituted nuclear program.

- Specific projects, with significant development, such as the efforts to build a rail gun and a copper vapor laser could have been useful in a future effort to restart a nuclear weapons program, but ISG found no indications of such purpose. As funding for the MIC and the IAEC increased after the introduction of the Oil-for-Food program, there was some growth in programs that involved former nuclear weapons scientists and engineers.

- The Regime prevented scientists from the former nuclear weapons program from leaving either their jobs or Iraq. Moreover, in the late 1990s, personnel from both MIC and the IAEC received significant pay raises in a bid to retain them, and the Regime undertook new investments in university research in a bid to ensure that Iraq retained technical knowledge.

Chemical

Key Findings

Saddam never abandoned his intentions to resume a CW effort when sanctions were lifted and conditions were judged favorable:

- Saddam and many Iraqis regarded CW as a proven weapon against an enemy's superior numerical strength, a weapon that had saved the nation at least once already—during the Iran-Iraq war—and contributed to deterring the Coalition in 1991 from advancing to Baghdad.

While a small number of old, abandoned chemical munitions have been discovered, ISG judges that Iraq unilaterally destroyed its undeclared chemical weapons stockpile in 1991. There are no credible indications that Baghdad resumed production of chemical munitions thereafter, a policy ISG attributes to Baghdad's desire to see sanctions lifted, or rendered ineffectual, or its fear of force against it should WMD be discovered.

- The scale of the Iraqi conventional munitions stockpile, among other factors, precluded an examination of the entire stockpile; however, ISG inspected sites judged most likely associated with possible storage or deployment of chemical weapons.

Iraq's CW program was crippled by the Gulf war and the legitimate chemical industry, which suffered under sanctions, only began to recover in the mid-1990s. Subsequent changes in the management of key military and civilian organizations, followed by an influx of funding and resources, provided Iraq with the ability to reinvigorate its industrial base.

- Poor policies and management in the early 1990s left the Military Industrial Commission (MIC) financially unsound and in a state of almost complete disarray.

- Saddam implemented a number of changes to the Regime's organizational and programmatic structures after the departure of Husayn Kamil.

- Iraq's acceptance of the Oil-for-Food (OFF) program was the foundation of Iraq's economic recovery and sparked a flow of illicitly diverted funds that could be applied to projects for Iraq's chemical industry.

The way Iraq organized its chemical industry after the mid-1990s allowed it to conserve the knowledge-base needed to restart a CW program, conduct a modest amount of dual-use research, and partially recover from the decline of its production capability caused by the effects of the Gulf war and UN-sponsored destruction and sanctions. Iraq implemented a rigorous and formalized system of nationwide research and production of chemicals, but ISG will not be able to resolve whether Iraq intended the system to underpin any CW-related efforts.

- The Regime employed a cadre of trained and experienced researchers, production managers, and weaponization experts from the former CW program.

- Iraq began implementing a range of indigenous chemical production projects in 1995 and 1996. Many of these projects, while not weapons-related, were designed to improve Iraq's infrastructure, which would have enhanced Iraq's ability to produce CW agents if the scaled-up production processes were implemented.

- Iraq had an effective system for the procurement of items that Iraq was not allowed to acquire due to sanctions. ISG found no evidence that this system was used to acquire precursor chemicals in bulk; however documents indicate that dual-use laboratory equipment and chemicals were acquired through this system.

*Iraq constructed a number of new plants starting in the mid-1990s that enhanced its chemical infra-
structure, although its overall industry had not fully recovered from the effects of sanctions, and had not
regained pre-1991 technical sophistication or production capabilities prior to Operation Iraqi Freedom
(OIF).*

- ISG did not discover chemical process or production units configured to produce key precursors or CW
  agents. However, site visits and debriefs revealed that Iraq maintained its ability for reconfiguring and
  'making-do' with available equipment as substitutes for sanctioned items.

- ISG judges, based on available chemicals, infrastructure, and scientist debriefings, that Iraq at OIF probably
  had a capability to produce large quantities of sulfur mustard within three to six months.

- A former nerve agent expert indicated that Iraq retained the capability to produce nerve agent in significant
  quantities within two years, given the import of required phosphorous precursors. However, we have no
  credible indications that Iraq acquired or attempted to acquire large quantities of these chemicals through its
  existing procurement networks for sanctioned items.

In addition to new investment in its industry, Iraq was able to monitor the location and use of all existing dual-
use process equipment. This provided Iraq the ability to rapidly reallocate key equipment for proscribed activities, if required by the Regime.

- One effect of UN monitoring was to implement a national level control system for important dual-use process plants.

*Iraq's historical ability to implement simple solutions to weaponization challenges allowed Iraq to retain the
capability to weaponize CW agent when the need arose. Because of the risk of discovery and consequences
for ending UN sanctions, Iraq would have significantly jeopardized its chances of having sanctions lifted or
no longer enforced if the UN or foreign entity had discovered that Iraq had undertaken any weaponization
activities.*

- ISG has uncovered hardware at a few military depots, which suggests that Iraq may have prototyped experi-
  mental CW rounds. The available evidence is insufficient to determine the nature of the effort or the time-
  frame of activities.

- Iraq could indigenously produce a range of conventional munitions, throughout the 1990s, many of which
  had previously been adapted for filling with CW agent. However, ISG has found ambiguous evidence of
  weaponization activities.

*Saddam's Leadership Defense Plan consisted of a tactical doctrine taught to all Iraqi officers and included
the concept of a "red-line" or last line of defense.* However, ISG has no information that the plan ever
included a trigger for CW use.

- Despite reported high-level discussions about the use of chemical weapons in the defense of Iraq, information acquired after OIF does not confirm the inclusion of CW in Iraq's tactical planning for OIF. We believe
  these were mostly theoretical discussions and do not imply the existence of undiscovered CW munitions.

*Discussions concerning WMD, particularly leading up to OIF, would have been highly compartmentalized
within the Regime. ISG found no credible evidence that any field elements knew about plans for CW use
during Operation Iraqi Freedom.*

- Uday—head of the Fedayeen Saddam—attempted to obtain chemical weapons for use during OIF, according to reporting, but ISG found no evidence that Iraq ever came into possession of any CW weapons.

ISG uncovered information that the Iraqi Intelligence Service (IIS) maintained throughout 1991 to 2003 a set of undeclared covert laboratories to research and test various chemicals and poisons, primarily for intelligence operations. The network of laboratories could have provided an ideal, compartmented platform from which to continue CW agent R&D or small-scale production efforts, but we have no indications this was planned. (See Annex A.)

- ISG has no evidence that IIS Directorate of Criminology (M16) scientists were producing CW or BW agents in these laboratories. However, sources indicate that M16 was planning to produce several CW agents including sulfur mustard, nitrogen mustard, and Sarin.

- Exploitations of IIS laboratories, safe houses, and disposal sites revealed no evidence of CW-related research or production, however many of these sites were either sanitized by the Regime or looted prior to OIF. Interviews with key IIS officials within and outside of M16 yielded very little information about the IIS' activities in this area.

- The existence, function, and purpose of the laboratories were never declared to the UN.

- The IIS program included the use of human subjects for testing purposes.

ISG investigated a series of key pre-OIF indicators involving the possible movement and storage of chemical weapons, focusing on 11 major depots assessed to have possible links to CW. A review of documents, interviews, available reporting, and site exploitations revealed alternate, plausible explanations for activities noted prior to OIF which, at the time, were believed to be CW-related.

- ISG investigated pre-OIF activities at Musayyib Ammunition Storage Depot—the storage site that was judged to have the strongest link to CW. An extensive investigation of the facility revealed that there was no CW activity, unlike previously assessed.

Biological

Key Findings

The Biological Warfare (BW) program was born of the Iraqi Intelligence Service (IIS) and this service retained its connections with the program either directly or indirectly throughout its existence.

- The IIS provided the BW program with security and participated in biological research, probably for its own purposes, from the beginning of Iraq's BW effort in the early 1970s until the final days of Saddam Husayn's Regime.

In 1991, Saddam Husayn regarded BW as an integral element of his arsenal of WMD weapons, and would have used it if the need arose.

- At a meeting of the Iraqi leadership immediately prior to the Gulf war in 1991, Saddam Husayn personally authorized the use of BW weapons against Israel, Saudi Arabia and US forces. Although the exact nature of the circumstances that would trigger use was not spelled out, they would appear to be a threat to the leadership itself or the US resorting to *"unconventional harmful types of weapons."*

- Saddam envisaged all-out use. For example, all Israeli cities were to be struck and all the BW weapons at his disposal were to be used. Saddam specified that the *"many years"* agents, presumably anthrax spores, were to be employed against his foes.

ISG judges that Iraq's actions between 1991 and 1996 demonstrate that the state intended to preserve its BW capability and return to a steady, methodical progress toward a mature BW program when and if the opportunity arose.

- ISG assesses that in 1991, Iraq clung to the objective of gaining war-winning weapons with the strategic intention of achieving the ability to project its power over much of the Middle East and beyond. Biological weapons were part of that plan. With an eye to the future and aiming to preserve some measure of its BW capability, Baghdad in the years immediately after Desert Storm sought to save what it could of its BW infrastructure and covertly continue BW research, hide evidence of that and earlier efforts, and dispose of its existing weapons stocks.

- From 1992 to 1994, Iraq greatly expanded the capability of its Al Hakam facility. Indigenously produced 5 cubic meter fermentors were installed, electrical and water utilities were expanded, and massive new construction to house its desired 50 cubic meter fermentors were completed.

- With the economy at rock bottom in late 1995, ISG judges that Baghdad abandoned its existing BW program in the belief that it constituted a potential embarrassment, whose discovery would undercut Baghdad's ability to reach its overarching goal of obtaining relief from UN sanctions.

In practical terms, with the destruction of the Al Hakam facility, Iraq abandoned its ambition to obtain advanced BW weapons quickly. ISG found no direct evidence that Iraq, after 1996, had plans for a new BW program or was conducting BW-specific work for military purposes. Indeed, from the mid-1990s, despite evidence of continuing interest in nuclear and chemical weapons, there appears to be a complete absence of discussion or even interest in BW at the Presidential level.

Iraq would have faced great difficulty in re-establishing an effective BW agent production capability. Nevertheless, after 1996 Iraq still had a significant dual-use capability—some declared—readily useful for BW if the Regime chose to use it to pursue a BW program. Moreover, Iraq still possessed its most important BW asset, the scientific know-how of its BW cadre.

- Any attempt to create a new BW program after 1996 would have encountered a range of major hurdles. The years following Desert Storm wrought a steady degradation of Iraq's industrial base: new equipment and spare parts for existing machinery became difficult and expensive to obtain, standards of maintenance declined, staff could not receive training abroad, and foreign technical assistance was almost impossible to get. Additionally, Iraq's infrastructure and public utilities were crumbling. New large projects, particularly if they required special foreign equipment and expertise, would attract international attention. UN monitoring of dual-use facilities up to the end of 1998, made their use for clandestine purpose complicated and risk laden.

Depending on its scale, Iraq could have re-established an elementary BW program within a few weeks to a few months of a decision to do so, but ISG discovered no indications that the Regime was pursuing such a course.

- In spite of the difficulties noted above, a BW capability is technically the easiest WMD to attain. Although equipment and facilities were destroyed under UN supervision in 1996, Iraq retained technical BW know-how through the scientists that were involved in the former program. ISG has also identified civilian facilities and equipment in Iraq that have dual-use application that could be used for the production of agent.

ISG judges that in 1991 and 1992, Iraq appears to have destroyed its undeclared stocks of BW weapons and probably destroyed remaining holdings of bulk BW agent. However ISG lacks evidence to document complete destruction. Iraq retained some BW-related seed stocks until their discovery after Operation Iraqi Freedom (OIF).

- After the passage of UN Security Council Resolution (UNSCR) 687 in April 1991, Iraqi leaders decided not to declare the offensive BW program and in consequence ordered all evidence of the program erased. Iraq declared that BW program personnel sanitized the facilities and destroyed the weapons and their contents.

- Iraq declared the possession of 157 aerial bombs and 25 missile warheads containing BW agent. ISG assesses that the evidence for the original number of bombs is uncertain. ISG judges that Iraq clandestinely destroyed at least 132 bombs and 25 missiles. ISG continued the efforts of the UN at the destruction site but found no remnants of further weapons. This leaves the possibility that the fragments of up to 25 bombs may remain undiscovered. Of these, any that escaped destruction would probably now only contain degraded agent.

- ISG does not have a clear account of bulk agent destruction. Official Iraqi sources and BW personnel, state that Al Hakam staff destroyed stocks of bulk agent in mid 1991. However, the same personnel admit concealing details of the movement and destruction of bulk BW agent in the first half of 1991. Iraq continued to present information known to be untrue to the UN up to OIF. Those involved did not reveal this until several months after the conflict.

- Dr. Rihab Rashid Taha Al 'Azzawi, head of the bacterial program claims she retained BW seed stocks until early 1992 when she destroyed them. ISG has not found a means of verifying this. Some seed stocks were retained by another Iraqi official until 2003 when they were recovered by ISG.

ISG is aware of BW-applicable research since 1996, but ISG judges it was not conducted in connection with a BW program.

- ISG has uncovered no evidence of illicit research conducted into BW agents by universities or research organizations.

- The work conducted on a biopesticide (*Bacillus thuringiensis*) at Al Hakam until 1995 would serve to maintain the basic skills required by scientists to produce and dry anthrax spores (*Bacillus anthracis*) but ISG has not discovered evidence suggesting this was the Regime's intention. However in 1991, research and production on biopesticide and single cell protein (SCP) was selected by Iraq to provide cover for Al Hakam's role in Iraq's BW program. Similar work conducted at the Tuwaitha Agricultural and Biological Research Center (TABRC) up to OIF also maintained skills that were applicable to BW, but again, ISG found no evidence to suggest that this was the intention.

- Similarly, ISG found no information to indicate that the work carried out by TABRC into Single Cell Protein (SCP) was a cover story for continuing research into the production of BW agents, such as *C. botulinum* and *B. anthracis*, after the destruction of Al Hakam through to OIF.

- TABRC conducted research and development (R&D) programs to enable indigenous manufacture of bacterial growth media. Although these media are suitable for the bulk production of BW agents, ISG has found no evidence to indicate that their development and testing were specifically for this purpose.

- Although Iraq had the basic capability to work with variola major (smallpox), ISG found no evidence that it retained any stocks of smallpox or actively conducted research into this agent for BW intentions.

The IIS had a series of laboratories that conducted biological work including research into BW agents for assassination purposes until the mid-1990s. ISG has not been able to establish the scope and nature of the work at these laboratories or determine whether any of the work was related to military development of BW agent.

- The security services operated a series of laboratories in the Baghdad area. Iraq should have declared these facilities and their equipment to the UN, but they did not. Neither the UN Special Commission (UNSCOM) nor the UN Monitoring, Verification, and Inspection Commission (UNMOVIC) were aware of their existence or inspected them.

- Some of the laboratories possessed equipment capable of supporting research into BW agents for military purposes, but ISG does not know whether this occurred although there is no evidence of it. The laboratories were probably the successors of the Al Salman facility, located three kilometers south of Salman Pak, which was destroyed in 1991, and they carried on many of the same activities, including forensic work.

- Under the aegis of the intelligence service, a secretive team developed assassination instruments using poisons or toxins for the Iraqi state. A small group of scientists, doctors and technicians conducted secret experiments on human beings, resulting in their deaths. The aim was probably the development of poisons, including ricin and aflatoxin to eliminate or debilitate the Regime's opponents. It appears that testing on humans continued until the mid 1990s. There is no evidence to link these tests with the development of BW agents for military use.

In spite of exhaustive investigation, ISG found no evidence that Iraq possessed, or was developing BW agent production systems mounted on road vehicles or railway wagons.

- Prior to OIF there was information indicating Iraq had planned and built a breakout BW capability, in the form of a set of mobile production units, capable of producing BW agent at short notice in sufficient quantities to weaponize. Although ISG has conducted a thorough investigation of every aspect of this information, it has not found any equipment suitable for such a program, nor has ISG positively identified any sites. No documents have been uncovered. Interviews with individuals suspected of involvement have all proved negative.

- ISG harbors severe doubts about the source's credibility in regards to the breakout program.

- ISG thoroughly examined two trailers captured in 2003, suspected of being mobile BW agent production units, and investigated the associated evidence. ISG judges that its Iraqi makers almost certainly designed and built the equipment exclusively for the generation of hydrogen. It is impractical to use the equipment for the production and weaponization of BW agent. ISG judges that it cannot therefore be part of any BW program.